GOD CAN SET YOU FREE FROM DEPRESSION

GOD CAN SET YOU FREE FROM DEPRESSION

Bishop Dr. William Wood
LLB(Hons)BL;Dip.MT;DM
(Solicitor–Advocate)

Wood World Missions Publications

Wood World Missions
238 - 240 London Road
Mitcham
Surrey,
CR4 3HD

Copyright © 2016 Bishop Dr. William Wood
Reprint 2018

All rights reserved. No part of this publication may be reproduced, stored in a retrieval system, or transmitted in any form or by any means, electronic, mechanical, photocopying or otherwise, without the prior written consent of the author.

ISBN-13: 978-1999919559

Printed in England

CONTENTS

Foreword 1

1. You Need the Joy of the Lord 3

2. Damaged Emotions 38

3. God Is Never Late 80

FOREWORD

Over the number of years that I have been serving the Lord, I have come to learn a few things about how important it is to maintain the joy that the Lord offers us in Christ Jesus. There are a lot of Christians who are always walking in sadness without realising that there is a joy in Christ Jesus that they could have.

Another thing that I have also learnt over the years is that a lot of people suffer from one form of depression or the other without knowing it.

It is the aim of this book, among other things, to educate ourselves on how we could come out of every depressive phase that the devil will have us walk in. I have done some research into this area and I am grateful to all those who have taught me things I never knew before some of which I have included in this book.

Lastly, I will like every reader to know that God is never late. What God has said about you and I is what he will do. Waiting time is never wasted time.

Stay blessed in Jesus name.

—Bishop Dr. William Wood

LLB(Hons)BL;Dip.MT;DM

CHAPTER 1

YOU NEED THE JOY OF THE LORD

Today, I see the Lord giving you a new identity in Jesus name. The Bible says " if any man be in Christ, he is a new creature, old things have passed away, behold all things have become new".

May the Lord give you something new today in Jesus name.

You need the Joy of the Lord.

Definition of Joy:-

"The emotion of great happiness ".

"To make glad or happy ".

"Full of high spirited delight ".

Today, may the Lord fill us up with high spirited delight in Jesus name.

1. John 10:10 " *The thief cometh not, but for to steal, and to kill, and to destroy: I am come that they might have life, and that they might have it more abundantly*".

You need to enjoy abundant life. That includes walking in Joy. Today, receive your joy in Jesus name.

2. Scriptural reasons why you need the joy of the Lord:- the Bible says:-

A.   Nehemiah 8:10

"*The joy of the Lord is our strength.* ".Nehemiah 8:10 says :- " Then he said unto them, Go your way, eat the fat, and drink the sweet, and send portions unto them for whom nothing is prepared: for this day is holy unto our LORD: neither be ye sorry; for the joy of the LORD is your strength".

A1. Psalm 105:4 says " *Seek the LORD, and his strength: seek his face evermore*".

B.

James 1:2 – 4 says *"My brethren, count it all joy when ye fall into divers temptations; knowing this, that the trying of your faith worketh patience. But let patience have her perfect work, that ye may be perfect and entire, wanting nothing"*.

C.

Psalm 30:5 says *"For his anger endureth but a moment; in his favour is life: weeping may endure for a night, but joy cometh in the morning"*.

D.

Hebrews 12:1-2

"Wherefore seeing we also are compassed about with so great a cloud of witnesses, let us lay aside every weight, and the sin which doth so easily beset us, and let us run with patience the race that is set before us, looking unto Jesus the author and finisher of our faith; who for the joy that was set before him endured the cross, despising the shame, and is set down at the right hand of the throne of God".

E.

Psalm 100:1 says "Make a joyful noise unto the LORD, all ye lands".

F.

Galatians 5:22-23 says "But the fruit of the Spirit is love, joy, peace, long suffering, gentleness, goodness, faith, Meekness, temperance: against such there is no law".

3.

John 15:11 says *"These things have I spoken unto you, that my joy might remain in you, and that your joy might be full."*

John 15:1-10 says "I am the true vine, and my Father is the husbandman. Every branch in me that beareth not fruit he taketh away: and every branch that beareth fruit, he purgeth it, that it may bring forth more fruit.

Now ye are clean through the word which I have spoken unto you. Abide in me, and I in you. As the branch cannot bear fruit of itself, except it abide in the vine; no more can ye, except ye abide in me.

I am the vine, ye are the branches: He that abideth in me, and I in him, the same bringeth forth much fruit: for without me ye can do nothing.

If a man abides not in me, he is cast forth as a branch, and is withered; and men gather them, and cast them into the fire, and they are burned.

If ye abide in me, and my words abide in you, ye shall ask what ye will, and it shall be done unto you. Herein is my Father glorified, that ye bear much fruit; so shall ye be my disciples.

As the Father hath loved me, so have I loved you: continue ye in my love.

If ye keep my commandments, ye shall abide in my love; even as I have kept my Father's commandments, and abide in his love.

4. Lack of joy produces depression.

Depressed people depress people.

Hurt people, hurt people.

Isolated people, isolate people.

But Delivered people, deliver people. Blessed people, bless people. Joyful people bring joy to people. Today, you shall be filled with joy in Jesus name. Today, you shall bring joy to those around you in Jesus name.

4a.

Definition of depression:-

Depression is:-

- "A mental state characterised by a pessimistic sense of inadequacy ".

- "A despondent lack of activity" in your life.

- "A state of depression can also be so severe as to require clinical and or divine intervention".

- "A sad feeling of doom and gloom".

- Today, may every spirit of doom and gloom come out of us in Jesus name.

4b. Comments:-

Effects of depression

1. Depression makes it tough for you to function as God would have you function.

2. Depression makes it difficult for you to enjoy life like you need to.

3. With depression, just getting through the day can be overwhelming; But, no matter how hopeless you may feel, you can get better.

4c. Bottom line.

Understanding the signs, symptoms and causes of depression is the first step to overcoming the depression.

4d.

Depression is not only attributable to the secular world, it is also attributable to the spiritual world.

You can:-

5. Be spiritual but depressed

6. Rich but depressed

7. Educated but depressed

8. Married but depressed

9. Have children but depressed

10. Have a Ministry but depressed

11. Anointed but depressed

12. Saved but depressed

13. Blessed but depressed

14. Working but depressed

15. Well-travelled but depressed

16. Be a great man or woman of God but depressed.

Note:-

Depression will present itself daily to all of us; but, we don't have to accept it; we don't have to entertain it and we don't have to fall for it.

We shall go for the Joy of the Lord in Jesus name.

5. *The Subtlety of Depression*

Depression is a very subtle reality. It manifests itself in all of us from time to time. Some more than others. Some much more than others.

Depression can ease itself into our daily lives and become our close companion without our knowledge or permission if we are not careful.

If given the chance, depression can begin to tamper with our minds and life perspective in such subtle ways that we soon forget what life was like before this "invasion by stealth" took place.

6. *Causes of depression*

17. Anxiety

18. Worry

19. Impatience

20. Feeling ignored

21. Feeling isolated

22. Feeling rejected

23. Feeling unfairly treated

24. Feeling excessively sad

25. Feeling overlooked

26. Having a Fear of the future

27. Feeling disappointed

28. Having a low self-esteem about yourself

29. Anger – example Cain

30. Jealousy – example Cain

31. Having severe feelings of disappointment

32. Loneliness

33. Lack of social support

34. Recent stressful life experiences

35. Family history of depression

36. Marital or relationship problems

37. Financial strain

38. Early childhood traumas or abuses

39. Alcohol or drug abuse

40. Unemployment or underemployment

41. Health problems or chronic pain.

Depression is:

- ✓ "A mental state characterised by a pessimistic sense of inadequacy ".
- ✓ "A despondent lack of activity" in your life.
- ✓ "A state of depression can also be so severe as to require clinical and or divine intervention".
- ✓ "A sad feeling of doom and gloom.

7.

Symptoms of depression:

If you identify with several of the following signs and symptoms, and they just won't go away, you may be suffering from clinical depression.

1) You can't sleep

2) You sleep too much

3) You can't concentrate or you find that previously easy tasks are now difficult

4) You feel hopeless and helpless.

5) . You can't control your negative thoughts, no matter how much you try

6) You have lost your appetite

7) You can't stop eating

8) You are much more irritable, short-tempered, or more aggressive than usual

9) You're consuming more alcohol than normal or engaging in other reckless Behaviour

10) You have thoughts that life is not worth living. You need to seek help immediately if this is the case.

11) Having Feelings of helplessness and hopelessness.

12) Having a bleak outlook of life and having a strong feeling that nothing will ever get better and there's nothing you can do to improve your situation.

13) Loss of interest in daily activities

14) Having no interest in former hobbies, pastimes, social activities, or even sex, if you are married.

15) You've lost your ability to feel joy and pleasure.

16) Having excessive Appetite

17) Significant weight loss or weight gain—a change of more than 5% of body weight in a month.

18) Sleep changes. Either insomnia, especially waking up in the early hours of the morning, or oversleeping also known as hypersomnia.

19) Anger or irritability. Feeling agitated, restless, or even violent. Your tolerance level is low, your temper short, and everything and everyone gets on your nerves.

20) Loss of energy. Feeling fatigued, sluggish, and physically drained.

21) Your whole body may feel heavy, and even small tasks are exhausting or take longer to complete.

22) Self-loathing. Strong feelings of worthlessness or guilt. You harshly criticize yourself for perceived faults and mistakes.

23) Reckless behaviour. You engage in escapist behaviour such as substance abuse, compulsive gambling, reckless driving, drinking or dangerous sports.

24) Concentration problems.

25) You have trouble focusing, making decisions, or remembering things.

26) Experiencing Unexplained aches and pains.

27) An increase in physical complaints such as headaches, back pain, aching muscles, and stomach pain are all signs and symptoms of depression.

8.

Warning signs of the fact that a depressed person is entertaining Suicidal thoughts.

1. They talk about killing or harming themselves.

2. They express strong feelings of hopelessness or being trapped.

3.   They have an unusual preoccupation with death or dying.

4.   They act recklessly, as if they have a death wish (e.g. speeding through red lights)

5.   They call or visit people to say goodbye.

6.   They get their affairs in order as if they were about to die. They start giving away their prized possessions in preparation for death.

7.   They say things like "Everyone would be better off without me" or "I want out" etcetera.

8.   They are unpredictable - they experience sudden switches from being extremely depressed to acting calm and happy - laughing one moment and crying the next moment.

9.

Q. *Is Suicide Hereditary?*

A.

We all have a past.

There may have been people in your past that entertained suicidal thoughts or even committed suicide. But we need to know that the Bible says " if any man be in Christ, he is a new creation, old things have passed away, behold all things have become new.

If we are a new creation in Christ and are determined to live this new life in Christ, our past can become history.

"History is not meant to be repeated, but to be learnt from..."

If we believe and accept the finished work of Jesus on the cross, history will not be repeated in our lives.

9.

How to Overcome Depression:-

1. Be determined to maintain your joy. Whatever you do, don't let anyone steal your joy.

2. Live in hope at all times. For the Bible says "hope deferred make the heart sick". Cultivate the habit of Laughing. Cultivate the habit of Smiling.

3. Pray and fast. Pray to the point where your praying turns into fasting. Pray until you are too busy praying to eat any food.

5. Do not forsake the assembly of the brethren as the manner of some is.

6. Study the word of God and apply the word of God that you study in your life - 2 Timothy 2:15

7. Find out what your vision in life is and seek to fulfil it.

Make healthy lifestyle Changes:-

8. Cultivate supportive relationships around you.

9. Get regular exercise and sleep. Have periodic rest. Even God rested.

10. Eat healthily - it will boost your mood naturally.

11. Manage effectively any stresses in your life and aim to eliminate them.

12. Practice relaxation techniques.

13. Challenge any negative thought patterns that come your way and get rid of them as soon as they come using the Word of God. For example Jesus did the same thing when he was tempted in the wilderness.

14. Q. *Are antidepressants right for you?*

Medication can help relieve the symptoms of depression in some people, but they aren't a cure and they come with drawbacks of their own. Learning the facts about antidepressants and weighing the benefits against the risks can help you make an informed and personal decision about whether medication is right for you.

15. If support from family and friends, positive lifestyle changes, and emotional skills building aren't enough, seek help from a mental health professional. There are many effective treatments for depression, including therapy, counselling, medication, and alternative treatments. Learning about your options will help you decide what measures are most likely to work best for your particular situation and needs.

16. Effective treatment for depression often includes some form of therapy/counselling. Therapy/counselling gives you tools to treat depression from a variety of angles. Also, what you learn in therapy/counselling gives you skills and insight to prevent depression from coming back.

17. Therapy/counselling can also help you work through the root of your depression, helping you understand why you feel a certain

way, what your triggers are for depression, and what you can do to stay healthy.

10. *The Road to Depression Recovery:-*

Just as the causes and symptoms of depression are different in different people, so are the ways to feel better. What works for one person might not work for another, and no one treatment is appropriate in all cases.

If you recognize the signs of depression in yourself or a loved one, take some time to explore the many treatment options.

In most cases, the best approach involves a combination of:-

- Social support,
- Lifestyle changes,
- Emotional skills building,
- Clinical help,
- Professional help,
- And divine help.

- Ask for help and support today in Jesus name.

Proverbs 3:5-6 says *"Trust in the LORD with all thine heart; and lean not unto thine own understanding. In all thy ways acknowledge him, and he shall direct thy paths"*.

11.

Examples of people in the word of God who were depressed.

A. Elijah after Mount Carmel.

1 Kings 19:1-4

"And Ahab told Jezebel all that Elijah had done, and how he had slain all the prophets with the sword. Then Jezebel sent a messenger unto Elijah, saying, So let the gods do to me, and more also, if I make not thy life as the life of one of them by tomorrow about this time. And when he saw that, he arose, and went (ran) for his life, and came to Beersheba, which belongeth to Judah, and left his servant there. But he himself went a day's journey into the wilderness, and came and sat down under a juniper tree: and he requested for himself that he might die;

and said, It is enough; now, O LORD, take away my life; for I am not better than my fathers".

B. King Saul was depressed and needed David to play a musical instrument to sooth his condition.

King Saul's condition has been known as "fits of morbid melancholia ".

I Samuel 16:14-23 *"But the Spirit of the LORD departed from Saul, and an evil spirit from the LORD troubled him. And Saul`s servants said unto him, Behold now, an evil spirit from God troubleth thee. Let our lord now command thy servants, which are before thee, to seek out a man, who is a cunning player on an harp: and it shall come to pass, when the evil spirit from God is upon thee, that he shall play with his hand, and thou shalt be well. And Saul said unto his servants, Provide me now a man that can play well, and bring him to me. Then answered one of the servants, and said, Behold, I have seen a son of Jesse the Bethlehemite, that is cunning in playing, and a mighty valiant man, and a man of war, and prudent in matters, and a comely person, and the LORD is with him. Wherefore Saul sent messengers unto Jesse, and said, Send me David thy son, which is with the* *sheep. And Jesse took an ass laden with bread, and a bottle of wine, and a kid, and sent them by David his son unto Saul.*

And David came to Saul, and stood before him: and he loved him greatly; and he became his armourbearer. And Saul sent to Jesse, saying, Let David, I pray thee, stand before me; for he hath found favour in my sight. And it came to pass, when the evil spirit from God was upon Saul, that David took an harp, and played with his hand: so Saul was refreshed, and was well, and the evil spirit departed from him".

B1.

1 Samuel 18:10-12

King Saul tried to kill David with a Javelin whenever the depressive mood kicked in.

"And it came to pass on the morrow, that the evil spirit from God came upon Saul, and he prophesied in the midst of the house: and David played with his hand, as at other times: and there was a javelin in Saul`s hand.

And Saul cast the javelin; for he said, I will smite David even to the wall with it. And David avoided out of his presence twice.

And Saul was afraid of David, because the LORD was with him, and was departed from Saul".

C. Cain and Abel.

Genesis 4:1-16 "*And Adam knew Eve his wife; and she conceived, and bare Cain, and said, I have gotten a man from the LORD.*

And she again bare his brother Abel. And Abel was a keeper of sheep, but Cain was a tiller of the ground.

And in process of time it came to pass, that Cain brought of the fruit of the ground an offering unto the LORD.4And Abel, he also brought of the firstlings of his flock and of the fat thereof. And the LORD had respect unto Abel and to his offering:

But unto Cain and to his offering he had not respect. And Cain was very wroth, and his countenance fell.

And the LORD said unto Cain, Why art thou wroth? and why is thy countenance fallen?

If thou doest well, shalt thou not be accepted? and if thou doest not well, sin lieth at the door. And unto thee shall be his desire, and thou shalt rule over him.

And Cain talked with Abel his brother: and it came to pass, when they were in the field, that Cain rose up against Abel his brother, and slew him.

And the LORD said unto Cain, Where is Abel thy brother? And he said, I know not: Am I my brother's keeper?

And he said, What hast thou done? the voice of thy brother's blood crieth unto me from the ground.

And now art thou cursed from the earth, which hath opened her mouth to receive thy brother's blood from thy hand;

When thou tillest the ground, it shall not henceforth yield unto thee her strength; a fugitive and a vagabond shalt thou be in the earth.

And Cain said unto the LORD, My punishment is greater than I can bear.

Behold, thou hast driven me out this day from the face of the earth; and from thy face shall I be hid; and I shall be a fugitive and a vagabond in the earth; and it shall come to pass, that every one that findeth me shall slay me.

And the LORD said unto him, Therefore whosoever slayeth Cain, vengeance shall be taken on him sevenfold. And the LORD set a mark upon Cain, lest any finding him should kill him.

And Cain went out from the presence of the LORD, and dwelt in the land of Nod, on the east of Eden".

D. King Saul consults a medium even though he had banned them from operating a few years earlier.

1 Samuel 28:3-25 "Now Samuel was dead, and all Israel had lamented him, and buried him in Ramah, even in his own city. And Saul had put away those that had familiar spirits, and the wizards, out of the land.

And the Philistines gathered themselves together, and came and pitched in Shunem: and Saul gathered all Israel together, and they pitched in Gilboa.

And when Saul saw the host of the Philistines, he was afraid, and his heart greatly trembled.

And when Saul enquired of the LORD, the LORD answered him not, neither by dreams, nor by Urim, nor by prophets.

Then said Saul unto his servants, Seek me a woman that hath a familiar spirit, that I may go to her, and enquire of her. And his servants said to him, Behold, there is a woman that hath a familiar spirit at Endor.

And Saul disguised himself, and put on other raiment, and he went, and two men with him, and they came to the woman by night: and he said, I pray thee, divine unto me by the familiar spirit, and bring me him up, whom I shall name unto thee.

And the woman said unto him, Behold, thou knowest what Saul hath done, how he hath cut off those that have familiar spirits, and the wizards, out of the land: wherefore then layest thou a snare for my life, to cause me to die?

And Saul sware to her by the LORD, saying, As the LORD liveth, there shall no punishment happen to thee for this thing.

Then said the woman, Whom shall I bring up unto thee? And he said, Bring me up Samuel.

And when the woman saw Samuel, she cried with a loud voice: and the woman spake to Saul, saying, Why hast thou deceived me? for thou art Saul.

And the king said unto her, Be not afraid: for what sawest thou? And the woman said unto Saul, I saw gods ascending out of the earth.

And he said unto her, What form is he of? And she said, An old man cometh up; and he is covered with a mantle. And Saul perceived that it was Samuel, and he stooped with his face to the ground, and bowed himself.

And Samuel said to Saul, Why hast thou disquieted me, to bring me up? And Saul answered, I am sore distressed; for the Philistines make war against me, and God is departed from me, and answereth me no more, neither by prophets, nor by dreams: therefore I have called thee, that thou mayest make known unto me what I shall do.

Then said Samuel, Wherefore then dost thou ask of me, seeing the LORD is departed from thee, and is become thine enemy?

And the LORD hath done to him, as he spake by me: for the LORD hath rent the kingdom out of thine hand, and given it to thy neighbour, even to David:

Because thou obeyedst not the voice of the LORD, nor executedst his fierce wrath upon Amalek, therefore hath the LORD done this thing unto thee this day.

Moreover the LORD will also deliver Israel with thee into the hand of the Philistines: and tomorrow shalt thou and thy sons be with me: the LORD also shall deliver the host of Israel into the hand of the Philistines.

Then Saul fell straightway all along on the earth, and was sore afraid, because of the words of Samuel: and there was no strength in him; for he had eaten no bread all the day, nor all the night.

And the woman came unto Saul, and saw that he was sore troubled, and said unto him,

Behold, thine handmaid hath obeyed thy voice, and I have put my life in my hand, and have hearkened unto thy words which thou spakest unto me.

Now therefore, I pray thee, hearken thou also unto the voice of thine handmaid, and let me set a morsel of bread before thee; and eat, that thou mayest have strength, when thou goest on thy way.

But he refused, and said, I will not eat. But his servants, together with the woman, compelled him; and he hearkened unto their voice. So he arose from the earth, and sat upon the bed.

And the woman had a fat calf in the house; and she hasted, and killed it, and took flour, and kneaded it, and did bake unleavened bread thereof:

And she brought it before Saul, and before his servants; and they did eat. Then they rose up, and went away that night".

E. Jesus at Gethsemane.

Matthew 26:36-46

"Then cometh Jesus with them unto a place called Gethsemane, and saith unto the disciples, Sit ye here, while I go and pray yonder.

And he took with him Peter and the two sons of Zebedee, and began to be sorrowful and very heavy.

Then saith he unto them, My soul is exceeding sorrowful, even unto death: tarry ye here, and watch with me.

And he went a little farther, and fell on his face, and prayed, saying, O my Father, if it be possible, let this cup pass from me: nevertheless not as I will, but as thou wilt.

And he cometh unto the disciples, and findeth them asleep, and saith unto Peter, What, could ye not watch with me one hour?

Watch and pray, that ye enter not into temptation: the spirit indeed is willing, but the flesh is weak.

He went away again the second time, and prayed, saying, O my Father, if this cup may not pass away from me, except I drink it, thy will be done.

And he came and found them asleep again: for their eyes were heavy.

And he left them, and went away again, and prayed the third time, saying the same words.

Then cometh he to his disciples, and saith unto them, Sleep on now, and take your rest: behold, the hour is at hand, and the Son of man is betrayed into the hands of sinners.6Rise, let us be going: behold, he is at hand that doth betray me".

Comment:-

- Depression presented itself to Jesus.
- Jesus prayed the perfect will of God into His life.
- Jesus was therefore able to overcome the depression.
- Today, I see you overcoming every depression that presents itself to you in Jesus name.

F. John the Baptist in prison.

Matthew 11:2-6 *"Now when John had heard in the prison the works of Christ, he sent two of his disciples,*

And said unto him, Art thou he that should come, or do we look for another?

Jesus answered and said unto them, Go and shew John again those things which ye do hear and see:

The blind receive their sight, and the lame walk, the lepers are cleansed, and the deaf hear, the dead are raised up, and the poor have the gospel preached to them.

And blessed is he, whosoever shall not be offended in me".

G.

Adam

Genesis 3:8-10 *"And they heard the voice of the LORD God walking in the garden in the cool of the day: and Adam and his wife hid themselves from the presence of the LORD God amongst the trees of the garden.*

And the LORD God called unto Adam, and said unto him, Where art thou? And he said, I heard thy voice in the garden, and I was afraid, because I was naked; and I hid myself".

You need the joy of the Lord.

CHAPTER 2
DAMAGED EMOTIONS

Summary of topics to cover:-

1. Some key introductory comments and remarks, scriptures and definitions relating to the Soul and Damaged emotions.

2. What are damaged emotions?

3. Causes of damaged emotions.

4. Symptoms of a person suffering from damaged emotions.

5. The 2 extremes of emotions that we need to stay away from.

6. Evidence of damaged emotions.

7. Examples of emotionally damaged people in the Bible.

8. How we can find healing for our damaged emotions.

1.

Introduction:-the Spirit, Soul and Body

Man is three(3) dimensional:-

1.   Is a Spirit

2.   Has a Soul - mind, emotions & will.

3.   Lives in a Body

The real you is your Spirit.

The Bible says "God is a Spirit and they that worship him should worship him in Spirit and in truth."

The Bible also says "we were created in the image and likeness of God". That tells me that we are Spirit beings first and foremost.

Our Emotions:- Our Emotions is one of the 3 parts of our SOUL. The other 2 parts of our Soul are our MIND and our WILL.

The Spirit:

When we get born again, our spirit gets born again. It's called justification - " just as if we have never sinned ".

Our Spirit is saved and is heading for heaven for as long as we remain saved.

The Bible says "...work out your salvation with fear and trembling...".

It's a daily affair.

We need to work it out in order for it to work for us.

The Bible says "They that endure to the end shall be saved."

I see you enduring to the end.

The Soul:-

We however need Sanctification in order for the process to be complete.

Sanctification is what gets our Soul in line with God's will in order for us to be saved in deed. Sanctification is what brings us to the place of truth.

The Body:-

As for the body, it will do what the Spirit & Soul influences it to do.

So if you and I are Justified and Sanctified, the body will always do what the justified and sanctified person asks them to do.

The story of Adam & Eve:-

The first response of Adam in the garden of Eden after he had sinned provides us with an insight into his emotions:

Genesis 3:8-10 "Then the man and his wife heard the sound of the LORD God as he was walking in the garden in the cool of the day, and they hid from the LORD God among the trees of the garden. But the LORD God called to the man, "Where are you?" He answered, "I heard you in the garden, and I was afraid because I was naked; so I hid."

Adam and Eve were hiding from the Lord. They were afraid. Fear came upon them. They saw themselves as naked.

For the first time, and certainly not the last, the emotion of fear was experienced by a human being. It led to Adam and Eve hiding from God. The damage was done. The emotional dimension of life would never be the same again.

Brethren, in order to see the glory of God in our lives, we need to Let God heal our damaged emotions.

Definition of Emotions:-

"Any strong feeling". It could be a positive emotion or negative emotion.

- ❖ Q. Why does a husband fight with his wife? Because of damaged emotions.

- ❖ Q. Why does a wife fight with her husband? Because of damaged emotions.

- ❖ Q. Why does a mother and father quarrel with their sons and daughters?

- ❖ Because of damaged emotions.

- ❖ Q. Why does a congregation member fight his Pastor? Because of damaged emotions.

- ❖ Q. Why does a Pastor fight with their congregation? Because of damaged emotions.

- ❖ Q. Why do some people dare to blame God for their difficult circumstances? Because of damaged emotions.

- ❖ Q. Why do some people divorce their wives and husbands? Because of damaged emotions.

....*Etcetera*

We all display feelings of emotion from time to time; it is normal to do so;

But, when that emotion is out of order it is referred to as Emotional Disorder & or Emotional Disturbance.

People who suffer from—*Damaged Emotions, Emotional Disorders* or *Emotional Disturbance* always have difficulties in building and keeping relationships.

Definition of Emotional Disorder & Emotional Disturbance:-

Emotional disorder is any mental disorder not caused by a detectable organic abnormalities of the brain, and in which a major disturbance of emotion is predominant". Suffering from Damaged Emotion is a mental disorder.

Today, it is my prayer that God will heal us from our damaged emotions in Jesus name.

Definition of Mental Disorder:-

Mental disorder is a psychological disorder of taught or emotion. Mental Disorder is a more neutral term than a mental illness.

Degrees of mental Disorder:-

1. Mild - moderate in type, degree or force.

2. Growing - on an upward trend

3. Severe - very strong or vigorous

4. Acute - extremely sharp and intense.

1.Some Scriptures:-

A. Matthew 9:12 "But when Jesus heard that, he said unto them, They that be whole (are well) need not a physician, but they that are sick".

B. Romans 12:1-2. "I beseech you therefore, brethren, by the mercies of God, that ye present your bodies a living sacrifice, holy, acceptable unto God, which is your reasonable service. And be not conformed to this world: but be ye transformed by the renewing of your MIND, that ye may prove what is that good, and acceptable, and perfect, will of God".

C.

Joel 2:25 says:- "… and I will restore to you the years that the locust hath eaten..."

D.

3 John 1:2 "Beloved, I wish above all things that thou mayest prosper and be in health, even as thy soul prospers".

It is God's desire that our soul (mind, emotions & will) prospers. After today, I see your soul prospering in Jesus name.

E.

Mark 3:35 "For whosoever shall do the will of God, the same is my brother, and my sister, and mother".

F.

2 Corinthians 10:4-6 "For the weapons of our warfare are not carnal, but mighty through God to the pulling down of strong holds; Casting down imaginations, and every high thing that exalteth itself against the knowledge of God, and bringing into captivity every thought to the obedience of Christ;

And having in a readiness to revenge all disobedience, when your obedience is fulfilled.

G.

Isaiah 43:18-19 "Remember ye not the former things, neither consider the things of old. Behold, I will do a new thing; now it shall spring forth; shall ye not know it? I will even make a way in the wilderness, and rivers in the desert".

H.

1 Corinthians 2:16 (Go for the mind of Christ) "For who hath known the mind of the Lord, that he may instruct him? but we have the mind of Christ".

After today, you shall have the mind of Christ.

2. *What Are Damaged Emotions?*

They are emotional feelings, responses and perspectives that are the product of wounds and injuries that have been done to our inner life. In more extreme cases, the emotional pain may have been so great that their memory has been suppressed to the point where there is no recollection of the occasion/s of the wounding.

1. Damaged emotions are "...scars of ancient painful hurts..." that causes us all kinds of interpersonal difficulties.

2. Damaged emotions are "A discolouration of a tragic stain that muddles one's life ".

3. Damaged emotions are "... Painful repressed memories which later explode into rage if not dealt with..."

4. Damaged emotions deeply affect our concepts, our feelings and our relationships.

5. Damaged emotions affect the way we look at life, at ourselves, at God

and at others.

6. Damaged emotions also affect the way we act if we are not careful.

Example - **The story of Cain** - *Genesis 4:1-16*

"And Adam knew Eve his wife; and she conceived, and bare Cain, and said, I have gotten a man from the LORD.

And she again bare his brother Abel. And Abel was a keeper of sheep, but Cain was a tiller of the ground.

3 And in process of time it came to pass, that Cain brought of the fruit of the ground an offering unto the LORD.

And Abel, he also brought of the firstlings of his flock and of the fat thereof. And the LORD had respect unto Abel and to his offering:

But unto Cain and to his offering he had not respect. And Cain was very wroth, and his countenance fell.

And the LORD said unto Cain, Why art thou wroth? and why is thy countenance fallen?

If thou doest well, shalt thou not be accepted? and if thou doest not well, sin lieth at the door. And unto thee shall be his desire, and thou shalt rule over him.

And Cain talked with Abel his brother: and it came to pass, when they were in the field, that Cain rose up against Abel his brother, and slew him.

And the LORD said unto Cain, Where is Abel thy brother? And he said, I know not: Am I my brother`s keeper?

And he said, What hast thou done? the voice of thy brother`s blood crieth unto me from the ground.

And now art thou cursed from the earth, which hath opened her mouth to receive thy brother`s blood from thy hand;

When thou tillest the ground, it shall not henceforth yield unto thee her strength; a fugitive and a vagabond shalt thou be in the earth.

And Cain said unto the LORD, My punishment is greater than I can bear.

Behold, thou hast driven me out this day from the face of the earth; and from thy face shall I be hid; and I shall be a fugitive and a vagabond in the earth; and it shall come to pass, that every one that findeth me shall slay me.

And the LORD said unto him, Therefore whosoever slayeth Cain, vengeance shall be taken on him sevenfold. And the LORD set a mark upon Cain, lest any finding him should kill him.

And Cain went out from the presence of the LORD, and dwelt in the land of Nod, on the east of Eden".

Other important Comments:-

1. Being born again and being filled with the spirit of God does not automatically take care of these damaged emotions.

2. Being spirit filled is not a short cut to emotional health.

3. Justification and Sanctification is the beginning of emotional health.

4. After we have become spirit filled, we need to patiently allow the holy spirit to work with us and in us in order to reduce and ultimately eradicate these damaged emotions.

5. We must be patient with people who have damaged emotions.

6. We must not judge them too harshly.

7. We must be patient with their confusing and contradictory behaviours.

8. We must keep away from unfairly criticising people who suffer from damaged emotions. They are not fakes, phonies or hypocrites.

9. They are people like you and I with hurts and scars and wrong programming that interfere with their behaviour.

10. Emotionally damaged people are simply put, sick people who need healing.

11. This is why we all need both Justification and sanctification in our lives.

12. It is impossible to know how Christian a person is merely on the basis of their outward look.

The bible says in Matthew 7:16 that: " ... by their fruits ye shall know them...".

"... by their deeds ye shall know whether they have damaged emotions or not ..."

"...by their roots you shall understand them and not judge them ...".

13. It is the Holy Spirit who will help us to:- de-programme, relearn and transform us from

all the past hurts into what God wants us to be.

Today, may the Holy Spirit help us to do this in Jesus name.

3. *WHAT CAUSES THESE DAMAGED EMOTIONS?*

These wounds and injuries have been caused by negative words, actions and attitudes inflicted upon us by 'significant others' - often in our childhood and formative years. These causes may be a single event of a traumatic kind or a pattern of abuse and destruction over many years.

The kinds of trauma that can have a negative impact can include the following:-

1. Rejection - having a sense of being unloved, unwanted, criticized or crushed.

2. Parental tyranny - loveless authority that crushes and abuses the spirit (Ephesians 6:4). *"And, ye fathers, provoke not your children to wrath:*

but bring them up in the nurture and admonition of the Lord".

3. Parental indifference - producing within the child a sense of worthlessness.

Example - The story of the Child with the grades - C, B & A.

The Story:

There was a school boy who always got "C" grades. When he showed the grade C to his parents, they said nothing. He then worked hard and started getting "B" grades. When he showed the grade B to his parents, they said nothing. He then worked hard and started getting "A" grades.

When he showed the grade A to his parents, his father said "those teachers always give "A" grades to undeserving pupils like you".

This comment affected the child for the rest of his life. The child needed clinical and divine deliverance in order to be set free from the emotional damage he suffered as a result of those comments by his parents.

4. Bereavement - significant loss through death or divorce.

5. Physical or Sexual abuse - painful memories that haunt the emotions and cripple your life. Sadly, many Christians bury the memories rather than face the pain. In doing so, they also bury the possibility of healing.

Some Christians struggle to face their pain because they believe that, now they are 'saved', they should no longer be afflicted by such realities as dysfunctional emotions.

4. *Symptoms of a Person Suffering from Damaged Emotions (Mental Disorder).*

WHAT ARE SOME OF THE SYMPTOMS OF DAMAGED EMOTIONS?

1. ***Defective Self-Image*** - feelings of inferiority, worthlessness and inadequacy. "I'm no good". "No one could accept me or love me". "God couldn't love someone like me".

2. ***Inappropriate Guilt*** - this person is always atoning, apologizing, doing more or trying harder. Satan uses this guilt to further accuse them and condemn them. They know little, if anything of the grace of God and the freedom of that grace.

3. ***Hyper-Sensitivity*** - these people are prisoners to the opinions of others. They are often very critical by nature because that's how they defend themselves from feelings of rejection. This leads to anxiety, withdrawal, tension and depression.

4. ***Fear of Failure*** - this person has been programmed by 'significant others' to both fear and expect failure.

The result is one of two extremes:-

1. They attempt everything with the hope of getting something right.

Or

2. They attempt little with the hope of getting nothing wrong.

5. ***Dysfunctional Relationships*** - damaged emotions make it difficult and in some cases impossible to relate to others healthily and appropriately (Remember the story of Adam and God). This has powerful implications for marriage relationships, families and Churches.

6. ***Repetitive Pattern of Defeat*** - all the good intentions and resolutions keep being sabotaged by cycle of:

Resolve, defeat, confession, rededication; resolve, defeat, confession, rededication – and the cycle goes on.

Two kinds of Christians are produced by this kind of treadmill experience:-

1. Those who are disillusioned.

The power of the gospel does not seem to work for them. They have no testimony of victory. So they despair. Some become bitter. They begin to pull away. Then they give it all away.

2. Those who are pretenders.

These people 'play the game'. They cover their fears and failures with a veneer of spiritual talk and activity and hope their real selves will go undetected.

Today, may the Lord heal our damaged emotions in Jesus name.

Other symptoms of damaged emotions:-

a) Always quarrelling

b) Always complaining

c) Always unhappy

d) Having mood swings

e) Always anxious

f) Never satisfied

g) Always envious

h) Always seeing things that others are not seeing

i) Always hearing things that others are not hearing

j) They are difficult to deal with

k) They are hurting people

l) They are always planning to hurt or destroy someone

m) They have a passion about what they are doing and what they are planning to do

n) They seek to gain converts to their course xxx

o) They have no teachable spirit

p) They are overbearing and very difficult to understand

q) They are very difficult to live with

r) They need help but are not convinced that they need help

s) They seek to hurt those who are helping them consciously or unconsciously.

t) They try to isolate themselves

u) They are suspicious of others

v) They are not the easiest people to persuade

w) They believe they are always right

x) They believe in themselves even when they are doing the wrong thing

y) They reject help when they need it the most

z) They seek to destroy anyone who goes all out to help them

aa) They are Always adamant and firm in their disobedient ways

bb) They are fixed in their ways

cc) They always like to isolate themselves from any potential source of help

Such People:

> Need prayer

> Need deliverance

- ➢ Need help
- ➢ Need you
- ➢ Need clinical attention
- ➢ Need God's divine intervention.

Today, it is my prayer that God will heal our damaged emotions in Jesus name.

5. The Two Extremes of Emotions That We Need To Stay Away From Are:

A. The concept that "anything that wiggles is the devil".

This is not always the case.

Don't blame the devil for everything that happens to you (or others).

It may be that the fault lies with you (or with them).

B. An overly simplistic syndrome which says that:- *Read your Bible, pray every day, have more faith, and all will be well with you. This is not always true.*

Speaking to people like this doubles the weight of their guilt and despair.

As Christians, we must always remember that giving over simplistic answers to people only drives them into despair and disillusionment - especially when things begin to go wrong in their lives.

6.*Further Evidence of damaged emotions:-*

The most common form of damage emotions:-

1. Having a deep sense of worthlessness.

2. Having a continuous feeling of anxiety, inadequacy and inferiority complex. Having an inner nagging that says:-

- "I am no good".

- "I'll never amount to anything".

- "No one could possibly love me".

- "Everything I do is wrong".

Such people when they become Christians sometimes have a feeling that God could not possibly love or forgive someone like them.

Their deep inner scars need to be touched and healed by the Holy Spirit.

4. The perfectionist Complex:-

They say things like:-

- ⊙ "I can't please myself".

- ⊙ "I can't please God".

- ⊙ "I can't please others".

- ⊙ "I never do anything well enough".

Such people are driven by inner ought's and should haves.

They say things like:-

"I ought to have done it differently".

"I should have done things differently" and so on. They are ever climbing but never reaching.

Today, whatever you are climbing, you shall reach your destination in Jesus name.

5. Super sensitivity.

(The super sensitive person).

1. The super sensitive person has usually been hurt deeply.

2. He reached out for love and approval and affection but instead he got the opposite and they have scars deep inside of them.

3. Sometimes, super sensitive people see things that other people don't see; and they tend to hear and feel things that others don't fell or hear.

4. They require constant appreciation, affirmation and approval.

5. You can never quite give them enough.

6. Sometimes, they seem very insensitive and sometimes even appear to be callous.

7. Sometimes they portray themselves to be hard and tough.

8. They sometimes want to get even and hurt others.

9. Sometimes, quite unbeknown to them, they spend their lives pushing people around, hurting them and dominating them.

10. They sometimes use money, authority, position, sex or even sermons to hurt people.

11. All this ends up affecting their Christian experience and that of those around them very deeply.

12. They are usually always afraid of losing something dear to them.

As a result, they always find excuses not to do things.

13. They live on "if only".

14. They never accomplish what they set out to accomplish.

15. They are always fearful and indecisive.

Today, may the Lord heal us of every supersensitive spirit in Jesus name.

7.

Examples of emotionally damaged people in the Bible:-

Eg. 1

King Saul and David.

1 Samuel 19:9-18

"And the evil spirit from the LORD was upon Saul, as he sat in his house with his javelin in his hand: and David played with his hand.

And Saul sought to smite David even to the wall with the javelin: but he slipped away out of Saul's presence, and he smote the javelin into the wall: and David fled, and escaped that night.

Saul also sent messengers unto David's house, to watch him, and to slay him in the morning: and

Michal David`s wife told him, saying, If thou save not thy life tonight, tomorrow thou shalt be slain.

So Michal let David down through a window: and he went, and fled, and escaped.

And Michal took an image, and laid it in the bed, and put a pillow of goats` hair for his bolster, and covered it with a cloth.

And when Saul sent messengers to take David, she said, He is sick.

And Saul sent the messengers again to see David, saying, Bring him up to me in the bed, that I may slay him.

And when the messengers were come in, behold, there was an image in the bed, with a pillow of goats` hair for his bolster.

And Saul said unto Michal, Why hast thou deceived me so, and sent away mine enemy, that he is escaped? And Michal answered Saul, He said unto me, Let me go; why should I kill thee?

So David fled, and escaped, and came to Samuel to Ramah, and told him all that Saul had done to him. And he and Samuel went and dwelt in Naioth".

Comments:

1. King Saul became emotionally damaged because of Jealousy.

2. He envied David.

3. He tried to kill David many times.

4. His damaged emotions gave him the condition called "Fits of morbid melancholia".

5. In the end he died a horrible death. May that never be your portion in Jesus name.

Eg. 2

Cain and Abel

Genesis 4:1-16 *"And Adam knew Eve his wife; and she conceived, and bare Cain, and said, I have gotten a man from the LORD.*

And she again bare his brother Abel. And Abel was a keeper of sheep, but Cain was a tiller of the ground.

And in process of time it came to pass, that Cain brought of the fruit of the ground an offering unto the LORD.

And Abel, he also brought of the firstlings of his flock and of the fat thereof. And the LORD had respect unto Abel and to his offering:

But unto Cain and to his offering he had not respect. And Cain was very wroth, and his countenance fell.

And the LORD said unto Cain, Why art thou wroth? and why is thy countenance fallen?

If thou doest well, shalt thou not be accepted? and if thou doest not well, sin lieth at the door. And unto thee shall be his desire, and thou shalt rule over him.

And Cain talked with Abel his brother: and it came to pass, when they were in the field, that Cain rose up against Abel his brother, and slew him.

And the LORD said unto Cain, Where is Abel thy brother? And he said, I know not: Am I my brother's keeper?

And he said, What hast thou done? the voice of thy brother's blood crieth unto me from the ground.

And now art thou cursed from the earth, which hath opened her mouth to receive thy brother's blood from thy hand;

When thou tillest the ground, it shall not henceforth yield unto thee her strength; a fugitive and a vagabond shalt thou be in the earth.

And Cain said unto the LORD, My punishment is greater than I can bear.

Behold, thou hast driven me out this day from the face of the earth; and from thy face shall I be hid; and I shall be a fugitive and a vagabond in the earth; and it shall come to pass, that every one that findeth me shall slay me.

And the LORD said unto him, Therefore whosoever slayeth Cain, vengeance shall be taken on him sevenfold. And the LORD set a mark upon Cain, lest any finding him should kill him.

And Cain went out from the presence of the LORD, and dwelt in the land of Nod, on the east of Eden".

Comments:-

Cain killed Abel because of Jealousy which developed into resentment, anger, bitterness, plotting and ultimately into deeply damaged emotions and violence.

May that never be your portion in Jesus name.

7.

How can we find healing for our damaged emotions?

How Do We Find Healing For Damaged Emotions?

1. Ask the Holy Spirit to reveal the real problem to you.

Dealing with symptoms will be short-term and unsuccessful.

Romans 8:26 states that the Spirit helps us in our weakness. We do not know what we ought to pray for, but the Spirit himself intercedes for us with groans that words we cannot express.

2. Face the damaged emotional area with honesty.

Stop denying your feelings and begin to own up to them.

Be authentic. Denial delays deliverance.

3. Ask yourself if you really want to be healed.

John 5:6.

When Jesus saw the man lying there and learned that he had been in this condition for a long time, he asked him, "Do you want to get well?"

We need to want to be healed in Jesus is to intervene and heal us.

4. Seek the support of someone you deeply trust.

You can't do this on your own.

James 5:14-16

The Bible says if there is anyone sick among us, they should call the elders of the church to pray over him and anoint him with oil in the name of the Lord. And the prayer offered in faith will make the sick person well; the Lord will raise him up. If he has sinned, he will be forgiven. Therefore confess your sins to each other and pray for each other so that you may be healed.

(Incidentally, the word translated 'sick' in v.14 is the same as translated 'infirm' or 'infirmities' or 'weakness' in other places in Scripture.

5. Acknowledge any responsibility you may have for what happened. However, don't accept responsibility or blame for what others may have done but want to blame you for.

6. Forgive the person or persons who wronged you. Refusal to forgive will weld shut the doors on your emotional prison.

7. Let Jesus become involved in your painful experience. He came to heal the broken-hearted (Isaiah 61:1) and His Lordship and Kingdom can extend over all of your life - including your emotional life.

8. Face your problems squarely. Face your problem with a ruthless moral honesty.

9. Acknowledge your problems to God and where possible to a trusted Christian for prayer support. Doing this will bring the inner healing that you need. (James 5:6).

10. Accept your responsibility in the matter. Stop blaming everyone else for what you are going through and accept your responsibility in the matter.

11. Ask yourself whether you want to be free. If yes, go for it.

John 5:6. Jesus asked the lame man "... do you want to be made whole ...".

12. Forgive yourself for your involvement in bringing about what you are going through. Forgiveness is an Act - do it. The fruits of forgiveness are in the Act of forgiveness.

13. Forgive everyone who is involved in your problem, hurt and damaged emotion.

Matthew 18:21-22 says:-*"Then came Peter to him, and said, Lord, how oft (how often) shall my brother sin against me, and I forgive him? till seven times?*

Jesus saith unto him, I say not unto thee, Until seven times: but, Until seventy times seven".

Matthew 18:23-35.

The Parable of the unforgiving servant.

"Therefore is the kingdom of heaven likened unto a certain king, which would take account of his servants.

And when he had begun to reckon, one was brought unto him, which owed him ten thousand talents.

But forasmuch as he had not to pay, his lord commanded him to be sold, and his wife, and children, and all that he had, and payment to be made.

The servant therefore fell down, and worshipped him, saying, Lord, have patience with me, and I will pay thee all.

Then the lord of that servant was moved with compassion, and loosed him, and forgave him the debt.

But the same servant went out, and found one of his fellowservants, which owed him an hundred pence: and he laid hands on him, and took him by the throat, saying, Pay me that thou owest.

And his fellowservant fell down at his feet, and besought him, saying, Have patience with me, and I will pay thee all.

And he would not: but went and cast him into prison, till he should pay the debt.

So when his fellowservants saw what was done, they were very sorry, and came and told unto their lord all that was done.

Then his lord, after that he had called him, said unto him, O thou wicked servant, I forgave thee all that debt, because thou desiredst me:

Shouldest not thou also have had compassion on thy fellow servant, even as I had pity on thee?

And his lord was wroth, and delivered him to the tormentors, till he should pay all that was due unto him.

So likewise shall my heavenly Father do also unto you, if ye from your hearts forgive not everyone his brother their trespasses".

Matthew 6:12 *"And forgive us our debts, as we forgive our debtors"*.

Unforgiveness produces:

- ➢ Resentment
- ➢ Anger
- ➢ Bitterness
- ➢ Hurt
- ➢ Strive
- ➢ Anxiety
- ➢ Negative reaction
- ➢ Pain
- ➢ Stress
- ➢ Conflict &
- ➢ All sorts of other emotional problems.

14. Ask the Holy Spirit to show you what your real problem is and how you need to pray about it.

Romans 8:26 *"Likewise the Spirit also helpeth our infirmities: for we know not what we should pray for as we ought: but the Spirit itself maketh intercession for us with groanings which cannot be uttered"*.

James 4:3 - pray the right kind of prayers.

15. Avoid having a low self-esteem about yourself.

Having a low self-esteem about yourself produces:-

- Frustration
- Anxiety
- depression
- More Hurt
- Feeling of abandonment
- Loneliness
- Isolation
- Rejection

- Worry
- Guilt
- Anger
- Doubt
- Hostility
- Psychological manipulation
- Having Feelings of inadequacy.

Today, Let God heal your damaged emotions.

Today, I see the Lord healing every damaged emotion in your life in Jesus name.

CHAPTER 3
GOD IS NEVER LATE

God will always be on time. God will make all things beautiful in his own time.

We need to understand the prophetic and Divine Timing of God in our lives.

Job 7:1 Is there not an appointed time to man upon the earth? Are not his days also like the days of an hireling (Hired man).

We need to know that there is an appointed time to our life. Our appointed time is set by God. Our appointed time is all in the Calendar of God. God is never late. God will always be on time.

Eg. 1

Luke 1:5-25: The story of Zachariah & Elizabeth

An angel appears to Zachariah.

Luke 1:5-25 *"THERE was in the days of Herod, the king of Judaea, a certain priest named Zacharias, of the course of Abia: and his wife was of the daughters of Aaron, and her name was Elisabeth.*

And they were both righteous before God, walking in all the commandments and ordinances of the Lord blameless.

And they had no child, because that Elisabeth was barren, and they both were now well stricken in years.

And it came to pass, that while he executed the priest`s office before God in the order of his course,

According to the custom of the priest`s office, his lot was to burn incense when he went into the temple of the Lord.

10 And the whole multitude of the people were praying without (outside) at the time of incense.

11 And there appeared unto him an angel of the Lord standing on the right side of the altar of incense.

12 And when Zacharias saw him, he was troubled, and fear fell upon him.

13But the angel said unto him, Fear not, Zacharias: for thy prayer is heard; and thy wife Elisabeth shall bear thee a son, and thou shalt call his name John.

14And thou shalt have joy and gladness; and many shall rejoice at his birth.

15For he shall be great in the sight of the Lord, and shall drink neither wine nor strong drink; and he shall be filled with the Holy Ghost, even from his mother`s womb.

16And many of the children of Israel shall he turn to the Lord their God.

17And he shall go before him in the spirit and power of Elias, to turn the hearts of the fathers to the children, and the disobedient to the wisdom of the just; to make ready a people prepared for the Lord.

18And Zacharias said unto the angel, Whereby shall I know this? for I am an old man, and my wife well stricken in years.

19And the angel answering said unto him, I am Gabriel, that stand in the presence of God; and am sent to speak unto thee, and to shew thee these glad tidings.

20And, behold, thou shalt be dumb, and not able to speak, until the day that these things shall be performed, because thou believest not my words, which shall be fulfilled in their season.

21And the people waited for Zacharias, and marvelled that he tarried so long in the temple.

22And when he came out, he could not speak unto them: and they perceived that he had seen a vision in the temple: for he beckoned unto them, and remained speechless.

23And it came to pass, that, as soon as the days of his ministration were accomplished, he departed to his own house.

24And after those days his wife Elisabeth conceived, and hid herself five months, saying,

25Thus hath the Lord dealt with me in the days wherein he looked on me, to take away my reproach among men.

Today, the Lord shall take away your reproach.

An angel appears to Mary. The promise of a Child.

Luke 1:26-56

And in the sixth month the angel Gabriel was sent from God unto a city of Galilee, named Nazareth,

To a virgin espoused to a man whose name was Joseph, of the house of David; and the virgin's name was Mary.

And the angel came in unto her, and said, Hail, thou that art highly favoured, the Lord is with thee: blessed art thou among women.

Ands when she saw him, she was troubled at his saying, and cast in her mind what manner of salutation this should be.

And the angel said unto her, Fear not, Mary: for thou hast found favour with God.

And, behold, thou shalt conceive in thy womb, and bring forth a son, and shalt call his name JESUS.

He shall be great, and shall be called the Son of the Highest: and the Lord God shall give unto him the throne of his father David:

And he shall reign over the house of Jacob for ever; and of his kingdom there shall be no end.

Then said Mary unto the angel, How shall this be, seeing I know not a man?

And the angel answered and said unto her, The Holy Ghost shall come upon thee, and the power of the Highest shall overshadow thee: therefore also that holy thing which shall be born of thee shall be called the Son of God.

And, behold, thy cousin Elisabeth, she hath also conceived a son in her old age: and this is the sixth month with her, who was called barren.

For with God nothing shall be impossible.

And Mary said, Behold the handmaid of the Lord; be it unto me according to thy word. And the angel departed from her.

And Mary arose in those days, and went into the hill country with haste, into a city of Juda;

And entered into the house of Zacharias, and saluted Elisabeth.

And it came to pass, that, when Elisabeth heard the salutation of Mary, the babe leaped in her womb; and Elisabeth was filled with the Holy Ghost:

And she spake out with a loud voice, and said, Blessed art thou among women, and blessed is the fruit of thy womb.

And whence is this to me, that the mother of my Lord should come to me?

For, lo, as soon as the voice of thy salutation sounded in mine ears, the babe leaped in my womb for joy.

And blessed is she that believed: for there shall be a performance of those things which were told her from the Lord.

And Mary said, My soul doth magnify the Lord,

And my spirit hath rejoiced in God my Saviour.

For he hath regarded the low estate of his handmaiden: for, behold, from henceforth all generations shall call me blessed.

For he that is mighty hath done to me great things; and holy is his name.

And his mercy is on them that fear him from generation to generation.

He hath shewed strength with his arm; he hath scattered the proud in the imagination of their hearts.

He hath put down the mighty from their seats, and exalted them of low degree.

He hath filled the hungry with good things; and the rich he hath sent empty away.

He hath helped his servant Israel, in remembrance of his mercy;

As he spake to our fathers, to Abraham, and to his seed for ever.

And Mary abode with her about three months, and returned to her own house.

Elizabeth gives birth to a son - and called him John.

Luke 1:57-80

Now Elisabeth`s full time came that she should be delivered; and she brought forth a son.

And her neighbours and her cousins heard how the Lord had shewed great mercy upon her; and they rejoiced with her.

And it came to pass, that on the eighth day they came to circumcise the child; and they called him Zacharias, after the name of his father.

And his mother answered and said, Not so; but he shall be called John.

And they said unto her, There is none of thy kindred that is called by this name.

And they made signs to his father, how he would have him called.

And he asked for a writing table, and wrote, saying, His name is John. And they marvelled all.

And his mouth was opened immediately, and his tongue loosed, and he spake, and praised God.

And fear came on all that dwelt round about them: and all these sayings were noised abroad throughout all the hill country of Judaea.

And all they that heard them laid them up in their hearts, saying, What manner of child shall this be! And the hand of the Lord was with him.

And his father Zacharias was filled with the Holy Ghost, and prophesied, saying,

Blessed be the Lord God of Israel; for he hath visited and redeemed his people,

And hath raised up an horn of salvation for us in the house of his servant David;

As he spake by the mouth of his holy prophets, which have been since the world began:

That we should be saved from our enemies, and from the hand of all that hate us;

To perform the mercy promised to our fathers, and to remember his holy covenant;

The oath which he sware to our father Abraham,

That he would grant unto us, that we being delivered out of the hand of our enemies might serve him without fear,

In holiness and righteousness before him, all the days of our life.

And thou, child, shalt be called the prophet of the Highest: for thou shalt go before the face of the Lord to prepare his ways;

To give knowledge of salvation unto his people by the remission of their sins,

Through the tender mercy of our God; whereby the dayspring from on high hath visited us,

To give light to them that sit in darkness and in the shadow of death, to guide our feet into the way of peace.

And the child grew, and waxed strong in spirit, and was in the deserts till the day of his shewing unto Israel.

Comments:-

God has heard our prayers, but, some answers to our prayers are tied to some prophetic and divine timings of God. We must continue to be faithful to God even when there is a delay in the physical manifestation of our answers. We must wait patiently for God's appointed time in our lives.

Elizabeth's miracle was prophetically and divinely tied to Mary's Miracle. Elizabeth had to wait for Mary to be born and for Mary to grow. Don't be moved by the comments of people.

Make sure your motives for wanting certain things from God are genuine motives.

Wait for the prophetic and divine timings of God in your life.

Your time is coming; don't corrupt your way. Still stay blameless before God.

There is a reason for everything. All things work together for good to them that Love God and are called according to his purpose.

Mary's miracle of a child was also prophetically and divinely tied to the timing of Simeon's death in Luke 2:25-35.

Luke 2:25-35

And, behold, there was a man in Jerusalem, whose name was Simeon; and the same man was just and devout, waiting for the consolation of Israel: and the Holy Ghost was upon him.

And it was revealed unto him by the Holy Ghost, that he should not see death, before he had seen the Lord's Christ.

And he came by the Spirit into the temple: and when the parents brought in the child Jesus, to do for him after the custom of the law,

Then took he him up in his arms, and blessed God, and said,

Lord, now lettest thou thy servant depart in peace, according to thy word:

For mine eyes have seen thy salvation,

Which thou hast prepared before the face of all people;

A light to lighten the Gentiles, and the glory of thy people Israel.

And Joseph and his mother marvelled at those things which were spoken of him.

And Simeon blessed them, and said unto Mary his mother, Behold, this child is set for the fall and rising again of many in Israel; and for a sign which shall be spoken against;

(Yea, a sword shall pierce through thy own soul also,) that the thoughts of many hearts may be revealed.

Mary's miracle of a child was also prophetically and divinely tied to Anna in Luke 2:36-40:

And there was one Anna, a prophetess, the daughter of Phanuel, of the tribe of Aser: she was of a great age, and had lived with an husband seven years from her virginity;

And she was a widow of about fourscore and four years, which departed not from the temple, but served God with fastings and prayers night and day.

And she coming in that instant gave thanks likewise unto the Lord, and spake of him to all them that looked for redemption in Jerusalem.

And when they had performed all things according to the law of the Lord, they returned into Galilee, to their own city Nazareth.

And the child grew, and waxed strong in spirit, filled with wisdom: and the grace of God was upon him.

Our thoughts and ways are not the Lord's thoughts.

Isaiah 55:8-13

For my thoughts are not your thoughts, neither are your ways my ways, saith the LORD.

For as the heavens are higher than the earth, so are my ways higher than your ways, and my thoughts than your thoughts.

For as the rain cometh down, and the snow from heaven, and returneth not thither, but watereth the earth, and maketh it bring forth and bud, that it may give seed to the sower, and bread to the eater:

So shall my word be that goeth forth out of my mouth: it shall not return unto me void, but it shall accomplish that which I please, and it shall prosper in the thing whereto I sent it.

For ye shall go out with joy, and be led forth with peace: the mountains and the hills shall break forth before you into singing, and all the trees of the field shall clap their hands.

Instead of the thorn shall come up the fir tree, and instead of the brier shall come up the myrtle tree: and it shall be to the LORD for a name, for an everlasting sign that shall not be cut off.

There may have been a delay to your miracle; but you need to know that there is a prophetic and divine reason for that delay.

Wait patiently for your Miracle. It shall surely come to pass.

The Benefits of Understanding the timing of God:

- It eliminates every anxiety in your life.
- It will give you rest.

- It will prevent you from being angry with God.

- Enables you to give praises to God well.

- It will keep you faithful in the things of God.

- It makes you stable in your walk with the Lord.

- It makes you joyful at all times.

- It makes you profitable to your generations.

- It gives you the peace of God even in the midst of your storms.

- It enables you to trust the Lord in the way that the Lord wants you to trust him.

- It makes you more committed to God.

- It enables you to serve God more consistently. It enables you to give towards God's work without struggling.

Q. *What is it that you have that was not given to you?*

Q. *Who is it that gave you the air you breath?*

Q. *Who is it that gave you the life you have?*

Q. *Who is it that gave you the strength you have?*

Q. *It is the Lord.*

- Understanding the prophetic and divine timing of God in our life, will enable us to give towards God's work without struggle.

- It brings you joy and laughter.

There is a time for everything.

Ecclesiastics 3:1-8 "To everything there is a season, and a time to every purpose under the heaven:

A time to be born, and a time to die; a time to plant, and a time to pluck up that which is planted;

A time to kill, and a time to heal; a time to break down, and a time to build up;

A time to weep, and a time to laugh; a time to mourn, and a time to dance;

A time to cast away stones, and a time to gather stones together; a time to embrace, and a time to refrain from embracing;

A time to get, and a time to lose; a time to keep, and a time to cast away;

A time to rend, and a time to sew; a time to keep silence, and a time to speak;

A time to love, and a time to hate; a time of war, and a time of peace."

Eg. 2

The Story of Abraham and Sarah

God is never late. God is always on time. May the Lord put laughter in your mouth. The dream that God gave to Abraham was linked to the future of the Children of Israel and to all of humanity.

Romans 4:19-25 *"And being not weak in faith, he considered not his own body now dead, when he was* *about an hundred years old, neither yet the deadness of Sarah`s womb:*

He staggered not at the promise of God through unbelief; but was strong in faith, giving glory to God; And being fully persuaded that, what he had promised, he was able also to perform. And therefore it was imputed to him for righteousness. Now it was not written for his sake alone, that it was imputed to him;

But for us also, to whom it shall be imputed, if we believe on him that raised up Jesus our Lord from the dead; Who was delivered for our offences, and was raised again for our justification.

Hindrances to us experiencing Joy and Laughter in our lives

If you believe that God is never late and that God is always on time, you will be able to overcome all the devices of the enemy aimed at stealing your joy and your laughter.

If God was never late for Abraham and Sarah, God will not be late for you.

Eg. 3

The Story of Joseph

Genesis 37:1ff.

Joseph's dreams were prophetically and divinely tied up to the prime ministerial position in Egypt and to Egypt's destiny and the destiny of the children of Israel.

Joseph's brothers took his garment of many colours.

What they did not realise was that:-

- The garment of glory
- The garment of favour
- The garment of righteousness

…and the garment of power was still upon Joseph.

The enemy may try and steal your physical garment but the enemy cannot take the garment that God gives to you unless you let him.

Joseph Rises to Power

Genesis 41:37-46 "And the thing was good in the eyes of Pharaoh, and in the eyes of all his servants.

And Pharaoh said unto his servants, Can we find such a one as this is, a man in whom the Spirit of God is?

And Pharaoh said unto Joseph, Forasmuch as God hath shewed thee all this, there is none so discreet and wise as thou art:

Thou shalt be over my house, and according unto thy word shall all my people be ruled: only in the throne will I be greater than thou.

And Pharaoh said unto Joseph, See, I have set thee over all the land of Egypt.

And Pharaoh took off his ring from his hand, and put it upon Joseph`s hand, and arrayed him in vestures of fine linen, and put a gold chain about his neck;

And he made him to ride in the second chariot which he had; and they cried before him, Bow the knee: and he made him ruler over all the land of Egypt.

And Pharaoh said unto Joseph, I am Pharaoh, and without thee shall no man lift up his hand or foot in all the land of Egypt.

And Pharaoh called Joseph's name Zaphnathpaaneah; and he gave him to wife Asenath the daughter of Potipherah priest of On. And Joseph went out over all the land of Egypt.

And Joseph was thirty years old when he stood before Pharaoh king of Egypt. And Joseph went out from the presence of Pharaoh, and went throughout all the land of Egypt.

Eg. 4

The Story of Hannah

1 Samuel 1:1ff.

Hannah's Miracle was prophetically and divinely tied to the nation of Israel.

Eg. 5

The Anointing of David as King

1 Samuel 16:1ff.

Why wasn't David anointed as king earlier? Why did God allow Saul to chase David to the point where David was sleeping in caves?

The Anointing of David delayed in coming, but it was prophetically and divinely linked to the better future that God had in store for his people.

Eg. 6

The story of David and Goliath

1 Samuel 17:1ff.

Eg. 7

The story of Dorcas

Acts 9:36-43

God is never late

God will always make sure that there is a Peter near Joppa, ready to come to your aid in your monument of need. You are on God's waiting list for your Miracle. God is never late. You are on God's waiting list for your Miracle.

Luke 1:5-25

Zachariah & Elizabeth

An angel appears to Zachariah.

THERE was in the days of Herod, the king of Judaea, a certain priest named Zacharias, of the course of Abia: and his wife was of the daughters of Aaron, and her name was Elisabeth.

And they were both righteous before God, walking in all the commandments and ordinances of the Lord blameless.

And they had no child, because that Elisabeth was barren, and they both were now well stricken in years.

And it came to pass, that while he executed the priest`s office before God in the order of his course,

According to the custom of the priest`s office, his lot was to burn incense when he went into the temple of the Lord.

And the whole multitude of the people were praying without at the time of incense.

And there appeared unto him an angel of the Lord standing on the right side of the altar of incense.

And when Zacharias saw him, he was troubled, and fear fell upon him.

But the angel said unto him, Fear not, Zacharias: for thy prayer is heard; and thy wife Elisabeth shall bear thee a son, and thou shalt call his name John.

And thou shalt have joy and gladness; and many shall rejoice at his birth.

For he shall be great in the sight of the Lord, and shall drink neither wine nor strong drink; and he shall be filled with the Holy Ghost, even from his mother`s womb.

And many of the children of Israel shall he turn to the Lord their God.

And he shall go before him in the spirit and power of Elias, to turn the hearts of the fathers to the children, and the disobedient to the wisdom of the just; to make ready a people prepared for the Lord.

And Zacharias said unto the angel, Whereby shall I know this? for I am an old man, and my wife well stricken in years.

And the angel answering said unto him, I am Gabriel, that stand in the presence of God; and am sent to speak unto thee, and to shew thee these glad tidings.

And, behold, thou shalt be dumb, and not able to speak, until the day that these things shall be performed, because thou believest not my words, which shall be fulfilled in their season.

And the people waited for Zacharias, and marvelled that he tarried so long in the temple.

And when he came out, he could not speak unto them: and they perceived that he had seen a vision in the temple: for he beckoned unto them, and remained speechless.

And it came to pass, that, as soon as the days of his ministration were accomplished, he departed to his own house.

And after those days his wife Elisabeth conceived, and hid herself five months, saying,

Thus hath the Lord dealt with me in the days wherein he looked on me, to take away my reproach among men.

Luke 1:26-56

An angel appears to Mary

And in the sixth month the angel Gabriel was sent from God unto a city of Galilee, named Nazareth,

To a virgin espoused to a man whose name was Joseph, of the house of David; and the virgin`s name was Mary.

28And the angel came in unto her, and said, Hail, thou that art highly favoured, the Lord is with thee: blessed art thou among women.

Ands when she saw him, she was troubled at his saying, and cast in her mind what manner of salutation this should be.

And the angel said unto her, Fear not, Mary: for thou hast found favour with God.

And, behold, thou shalt conceive in thy womb, and bring forth a son, and shalt call his name JESUS.

He shall be great, and shall be called the Son of the Highest: and the Lord God shall give unto him the throne of his father David:

And he shall reign over the house of Jacob for ever; and of his kingdom there shall be no end.

Then said Mary unto the angel, How shall this be, seeing I know not a man?

And the angel answered and said unto her, The Holy Ghost shall come upon thee, and the power of the Highest shall overshadow thee: therefore also that holy thing which shall be born of thee shall be called the Son of God.

And, behold, thy cousin Elisabeth, she hath also conceived a son in her old age: and this is the sixth month with her, who was called barren.

For with God nothing shall be impossible.

And Mary said, Behold the handmaid of the Lord; be it unto me according to thy word. And the angel departed from her.

And Mary arose in those days, and went into the hill country with haste, into a city of Juda;

And entered into the house of Zacharias, and saluted Elisabeth.

And it came to pass, that, when Elisabeth heard the salutation of Mary, the babe leaped in her womb; and Elisabeth was filled with the Holy Ghost:

And she spake out with a loud voice, and said, blessed art thou among women, and blessed is the fruit of thy womb.

And whence is this to me, that the mother of my Lord should come to me?

For, lo, as soon as the voice of thy salutation sounded in mine ears, the babe leaped in my womb for joy.

And blessed is she that believed: for there shall be a performance of those things which were told her from the Lord.

And Mary said, My soul doth magnify the Lord,

And my spirit hath rejoiced in God my Saviour.

For he hath regarded the low estate of his handmaiden: for, behold, from henceforth all generations shall call me blessed.

For he that is mighty hath done to me great things; and holy is his name.

And his mercy is on them that fear him from generation to generation.

He hath shewed strength with his arm; he hath scattered the proud in the imagination of their hearts.

He hath put down the mighty from their seats, and exalted them of low degree.

He hath filled the hungry with good things; and the rich he hath sent empty away.

He hath helped his servant Israel, in remembrance of his mercy;

As he spake to our fathers, to Abraham, and to his seed for ever.

And Mary abode with her about three months, and returned to her own house.

Luke 1:57-80

Elizabeth gives birth to a son - and called him Isaac.

Now Elisabeth`s full time came that she should be delivered; and she brought forth a son.

And her neighbours and her cousins heard how the Lord had shewed great mercy upon her; and they rejoiced with her.

And it came to pass, that on the eighth day they came to circumcise the child; and they called him Zacharias, after the name of his father.

And his mother answered and said, Not so; but he shall be called John.

And they said unto her, There is none of thy kindred that is called by this name.

And they made signs to his father, how he would have him called.

And he asked for a writing table, and wrote, saying, His name is John. And they marvelled all.

And his mouth was opened immediately, and his tongue loosed, and he spake, and praised God.

And fear came on all that dwelt round about them: and all these sayings were noised abroad throughout all the hill country of Judaea.

And all they that heard them laid them up in their hearts, saying, What manner of child shall this be! And the hand of the Lord was with him.

And his father Zacharias was filled with the Holy Ghost, and prophesied, saying,

Blessed be the Lord God of Israel; for he hath visited and redeemed his people,

And hath raised up an horn of salvation for us in the house of his servant David;

As he spake by the mouth of his holy prophets, which have been since the world began:

That we should be saved from our enemies, and from the hand of all that hate us;

To perform the mercy promised to our fathers, and to remember his holy covenant;

The oath which he sware to our father Abraham,

That he would grant unto us, that we being delivered out of the hand of our enemies might serve him without fear,

In holiness and righteousness before him, all the days of our life.

And thou, child, shalt be called the prophet of the Highest: for thou shalt go before the face of the Lord to prepare his ways;

To give knowledge of salvation unto his people by the remission of their sins,

Through the tender mercy of our God; whereby the dayspring from on high hath visited us,

To give light to them that sit in darkness and in the shadow of death, to guide our feet into the way of peace.

And the child grew, and waxed strong in spirit, and was in the deserts till the day of his shewing unto Israel.

If this book has blessed you in any way, shape or form, we will like to hear your testimony. Simply write your testimony and send it to us.

Our postal address in the UK is:
Wood World Missions & Power Centre Church,
238 – 240 London Road,
Mitcham, Surrey, CR4 3HD, United Kingdom.
E-mail:-
rev.dr.wood@hotmail.co.uk
or
woodworldmissions@hotmail.com
Website address:-
www.woodworldmissions.org
or
www.powercentrechurchuk.org
U.K.: Tel. No: (+44) 208 286 3018
Mobile: (+44) 7909 486 846
Ring any of the above numbers for information about the Wood World Missions' free Bible School in the United Kingdom.

www.ingramcontent.com/pod-product-compliance
Lightning Source LLC
Chambersburg PA
CBHW021013090426
42738CB00007B/773